GREETING CARD WISDOM

Insights and Inspiration from the Brush Dance
Greeting Card Collection

we do not remember DAYS; we remember moments.

Painting and Calligraphy by Renée Locks
Text by Marc Lesser

Brush Dance
Sausalito, California

To Harry Roberts, whose life
and story about the
Brush Dance healing ritual teaches
us to be true to ourselves and to
give our best.

Copyright © 2000 Brush Dance, Inc.
Painting and Calligraphy by Renée Locks
Text by Marc Lesser

All Rights Reserved. No part of this publication may be reproduced, stored
in or introduced into a retrieval system, or copied in any form without the
prior written permission of the publisher, except for review or citation.
For information, contact:

Brush Dance, Inc., 100 Ebbtide Avenue, #1,
Sausalito, CA 94965
www@brushdance.com

ISBN 1891731556

Printed in Korea
First Printing
GBREN01

CONTENTS

FOREWORD

Greeting Card Wisdom was inspired by the many people who buy Brush Dance cards — and never send them! Instead of being mailed, our cards are displayed on walls, on desks, or throughout people's homes as gentle reminders or affirmations — a way to see the world a little differently. Greeting Card Wisdom was also inspired by the people who wrote us to say that our cards had captured their sentiments, that we had expressed them in just the right way — to celebrate a special occasion, offer comfort and encouragement to someone who was grieving or in transition, or simply to make someone smile.

To better understand our customers, I often ask, Are you a greeting card buyer? Here's what I learned: I learned that women buy lots of cards and that quite often they store them in a shoebox! That way they always have a card available, whatever the occasion.

(Yes, men do buy cards — but not till the day they need them . . .)

Over the past 10 years, Brush Dance has evolved to become something more than a greeting card company. We design products that help people live their lives more deeply. Brush Dance designs and produces spiritual lifestyle products, products that help people be true to themselves.

In fact, the company name Brush Dance reflects both our mission and our story. On the back of each card we print the following:

The Brush Dance is a Yurok Indian healing ritual where being true to yourself means giving your best to help a person in need. Being true to yourself is the one and only Yurok Indian law.

So, while this is a book about greeting cards, it is more than that. This is a collection of wisdom — a tool for being true to yourself.

The day we met Renée Locks was a real turning point in the history of Brush Dance. It was the winter of 1989 and my wife and I had already started Brush Dance. We were printing beautiful wrapping paper and a few cards -- one of the first companies in the world to use recycled paper. Everyone told us that our products were beautiful and unique, but we only sold half the inventory we produced for our small mail order catalog. We decided to try selling our wrapping paper and cards at holiday fairs in the San Francisco Bay Area.

One of the first fairs we attended was a quaint, hometown fair in Mill Valley, California, minutes from the Golden Gate Bridge. A few booths down from ours we discovered the wonderfully talented artist Renée Locks. Renée's cards -- all of them made by hand -- combined exquisite watercolor paintings with the ancient Chinese art of sumi-brush calligraphy. They were so unique and engaging. Her words made us stop and think, smile, and sometimes nod in agreement. They touched our hearts.

We introduced ourselves, explaining that we had just started a publishing company and we were seeking artists. Renée showed us literally hundreds of her wonderful cards! She told us with pride that she had put all five of her children through high school and college by making and selling her handmade cards.

A few days later, when we were ready to discuss a working relationship, Renée invited us to her home. Everywhere we looked we saw her delightful cards -- in the living room, in the kitchen, in the bedrooms -- everywhere! We loved her work and her energy. She had vision. She was a delightful person. She poured us some hot tea, and as we sat in front of her fireplace sipping our tea, we began to work together.

Though our combined efforts are expressed in the form of greeting cards, the real work is in the particular combination of words and art, that unique synthesis of paper and paint, of minds and hearts that meet at play. We have discovered that the wisdom isn't in the cards -- it's in each one of us!

Marc Lesser, Sausalito, Ca.

RENÉE IN HER GARDEN

I NEVER SET OUT TO ILLUSTRATE GREET-ING CARDS. THE VERY FIRST CARDS I DID WERE HUNG ON MY BATHROOM MIRROR OR REFRIGERATOR DOOR AS A SILENT WAY OF COMMUNICATING NOURISHING MESSAGES TO MYSELF AND MY FIVE CHIL-DREN WITHOUT THEIR HAVING TO RESPOND.

THROUGH THE SUMI BRUSH, I EXPRESS MY LOVE OF AND RELATIONSHIP WITH NATURE. TO ME, THE LESSONS OF MOTHER NATURE ARE A NECESSARY PART OF OUR PHYSICAL, MENTAL, AND SPIRITUAL WELL BEING. IN OUR HECTIC TIMES, IT CAN BE HEALING TO LOOK AT A SINGLE BLADE OF GRASS OR A SINGLE FLOWER. I KNOW THE IMPORTANCE OF PEACE STARTING WITHIN EACH OF US. I WOULD LIKE MY LITTLE CARDS TO HELP US GET IN TOUCH WITH THAT PEACE.

BEFORE I DO ANY ARTWORK, I CENTER MYSELF TO FOCUS ON WHAT I AM DOING AND MY MEANING. I GET TO WITNESS THE MAGIC OF SEEING A FEELING MAN-IFEST. I HAVE BEEN PAINTING MOST OF MY LIFE, DOING CALLIGRAPHY FOR OVER 20 YEARS, DAILY REFINING AND PERFECTING WHAT I DO. I ALWAYS ASK MYSELF WHY AM I USING MY ART IN THIS FORM; IS THERE A NEED FOR WHAT IS BEING SAID; IS THERE A WAY TO EXPRESS WHAT I AM INSPIRED TO EXPRESS IN A WAY THAT WILL BE UNDER-STOOD AND ELEGANT? MY FOCUS IS CLARITY; THAT IS NUMBER ONE, WITH BOTH IMAGE AND WORD. I TRY TO GIVE EACH PIECE MY ALL AT THAT MOMENT. IF I AM NOT INTERESTED IN WHAT I AM DOING, WHY SHOULD I EXPECT ANYONE ELSE TO BE?

For me, wandering around with my art, exploring, trying something I haven't tried before is important, important for the new challenge, the new solution to be found, the element of surprise and magic. It's like taking the back road instead of the freeway. Whatever words I choose, I try to use with the awareness that words carry energy and that we are responsible for them.

I have taught calligraphy to young folks, and to women of means seeking ways to express themselves. I have also worked at a women's shelter and made cards they could hang there. Out of these experiences I have come to understand that there are certain feelings we humans, young and old, rich and poor, all share. If I did not think greeting cards were important I would not waste my time on them. That greetings fit so nicely on cards and can be shared with so many is what makes greeting cards important to me. Since meeting with Brush Dance, I am overjoyed that so much more can be shared with so many more folks.

I see greeting cards as mini-messages, vitamins for our eyes and our minds, more intimate than the phone or the Internet, because you can hold them in your hands and read them over and over. We all love and need to communicate with each other. Greeting cards are a way humans can do that.

Renée Locks

Let yourself be vulnerable; it's ok to not know.

It is no accident that this section appears first. All change, all growth, all healing comes from acceptance, acknowledging that we are vulnerable, realizing that we do not know. Where did we come from? Where are we going? Who is it that is doing this breathing and thinking? What will happen tomorrow or in the next moment? This vulnerability, this not knowing softens us, breaks down barriers and connects us all.

The great Zen teacher Dogen compared life to the act of rowing a boat. We are all in our own boats, being carried by the current of the river. But we do not control the river. We do not know where the river will take us. Our task is to simply paddle the boat and meet whatever comes, and to realize that we are all in the same river, being strengthened by not knowing what will happen next.

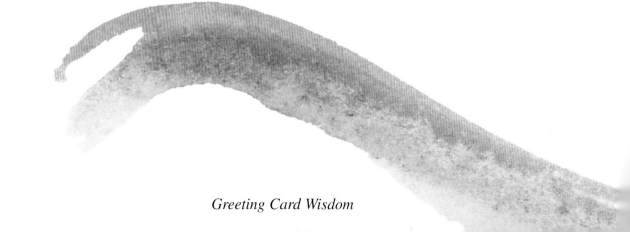

Greeting Card Wisdom

I enter
This
Day
with
A
Peaceful
Heart

Greeting Card Wisdom

We find
our way
one
step
at
a time.

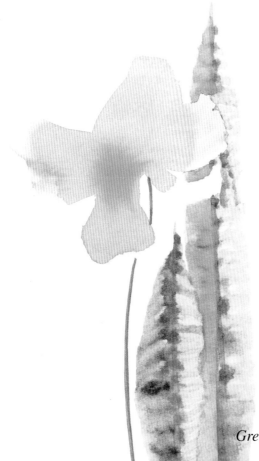

when
one door
closes,
another
one
opens...
somewhere

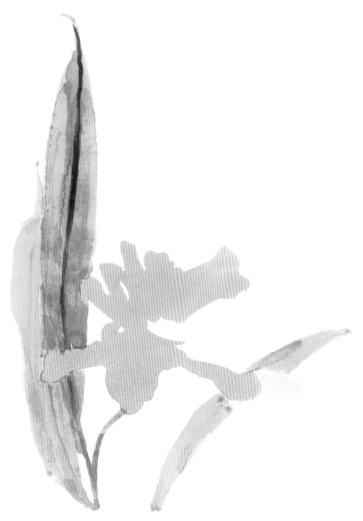

Life would
be infinitely
happier if
we could
be born at
The Age of 80
And gradually
Approach 18.

Trust Yourself.

Our lives are full of paradox. How do we practice not knowing and at the same time practice trusting ourselves? Going back to Dogen's metaphor of rowing the boat, we must trust our ability to row our boat as best we can. We can use and trust our senses, our bodies, and our experiences. We can be still enough and quiet enough to see and feel what is really happening in our lives, as well as begin to understand what is happening in the lives of others.

Each time we create a greeting card we are faced with this paradox of trust. Do the words we choose have power? Is this the best image to go with these words? Why would someone send this card? Our market research is what our hearts tell us. We never really know how the card will be received. Part of trusting ourselves is trusting our process -- making our best effort each time, listening and watching, learning from each failure and each success.

Greeting Card Wisdom

JUST
TRUST
YOURSELF.
THEN
YOU
WILL
KNOW
HOW
TO
LIVE.

-GOETHE

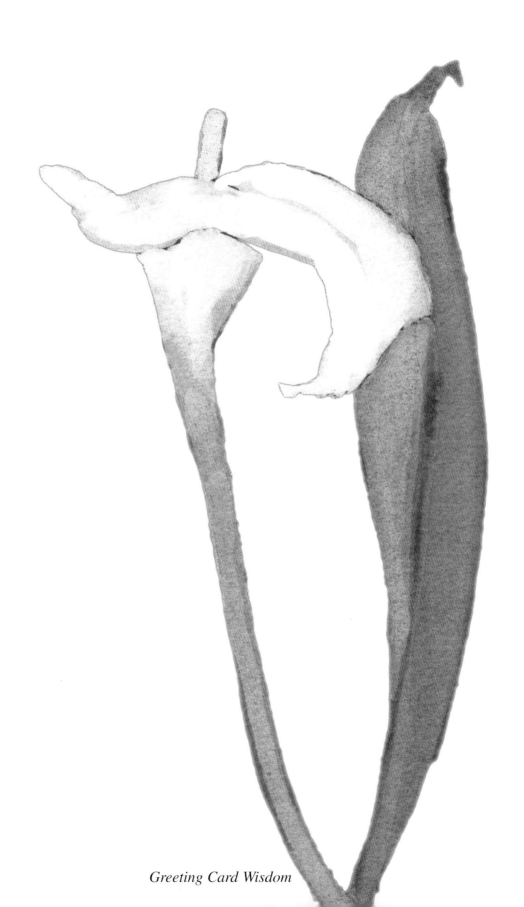

Greeting Card Wisdom

We cannot
direct
the wind
but we can
Adjust
our sails.

The future belongs
to those
who believe
in the beauty
of their
Dreams.

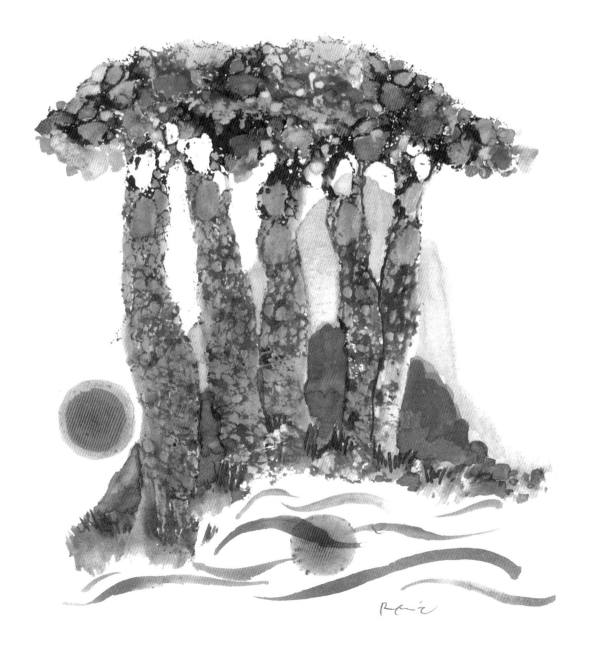

The challenge
is to be
yourself
in a
world
that is
trying
to
make
you
like
everyone
else

It isn't the mountains ahead that wear you out. It's the grain of sand in your shoe.

Cultivate an open, flexible mind.

OUR HABITS AND PATTERNS AND THE WAYS WE BECOME ACCUSTOMED TO SEEING OURSELVES, OTHERS, AND THE WORLD, ARE DIFFICULT TO CHANGE. GROWING BRUSH DANCE AS A BUSINESS PROVIDES US WITH AN EXCELLENT OPPORTUNITY TO TEST AND DEVELOP OUR FLEXIBILITY. BRUSH DANCE BEGAN IN 1989 AS A SMALL MAIL ORDER CATALOG SELLING ENVIRONMENTAL PRODUCTS. A FEW YEARS LATER, DUE TO THE RESPONSE OF OUR CUSTOMERS, WE BECAME A WHOLESALE PUBLISHER OF GREETING CARDS.

MORE RECENTLY, WE HAVE COME TO REALIZE THAT OUR MISSION IS TO BE A PUBLISHER OF SPIRITUAL PRODUCTS. TODAY, WE ARE EXPANDING INTO E-COMMERCE, AS WE OFFER A WHOLE LINE OF SPIRITUAL LIFESTYLE PRODUCTS AND RESOURCES OVER THE INTERNET IN ADDITION TO BEING A WHOLESALE PUBLISHING COMPANY.

IN THE CLASSIC ZEN MIND, BEGINNER'S MIND, SHUNRYU SUZUKI SAYS, IT IS THE READINESS OF MIND THAT IS WISDOM.

Greeting Card Wisdom

What people really need is a good listening to.

MARY
LOU
CASEY

Luck is
being
prepared
for

Opportunity
when it
comes.

CITY OF HOPE

I dwell in possibility

EMILY DICKINSON

Take
A
Little
Quiet
Time
Every
Day

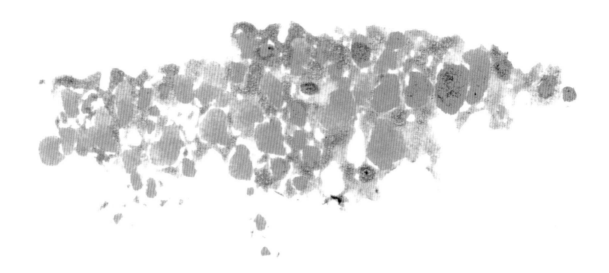

Nothing
is
worth more
than this
day.

Life is short

THE GREAT ZEN TEACHER DOGEN WAS DRAMATI-
CALLY AFFECTED BY THE DEATH OF HIS MOTHER WHEN HE
WAS NINE YEARS OLD. IT IS SAID HE WAS SITTING NEAR HIS
MOTHER'S BODY BEFORE THE FUNERAL. AND AS HE
WATCHED THE SMOKE FROM THE INCENSE RISE AND FLOAT
INTO THE AIR, THEN FADE AND DISAPPEAR, HE REALIZED
THAT LIFE WAS FLEETING LIKE THE SMOKE THAT ROSE ABOVE
HIS MOTHER'S BODY, APPEARING BRIEFLY, THEN FADING AND
DISAPPEARING. THIS EXPERIENCE SHAPED HIS INTENTION TO
DEVOTE HIS LIFE TO PENETRATING THE PROFOUND QUESTIONS
OF LIFE AND DEATH.

IN ZEN MONASTERIES A WOODEN MALLET IS USED TO
STRIKE A WOODEN BOARD TO ANNOUNCE MEDITATION
PRACTICE. WRITTEN ON THE BACK OF THE BOARD ARE THE
WORDS:

AWAKE! AWAKE!
LIFE AND DEATH ARE THE GREAT MATTERS.
DON'T WASTE TIME.

Greeting Card Wisdom

Life
is too
short
to
wear
tight
shoes

GRANDMA ROS

If I've got
    to
    age
I'm going
    to age
magnificently!

Greeting Card Wisdom

You cannot do
a kindness
too soon
because you
never know
how soon
will be
too late.

RALPH WALDO
EMERSON

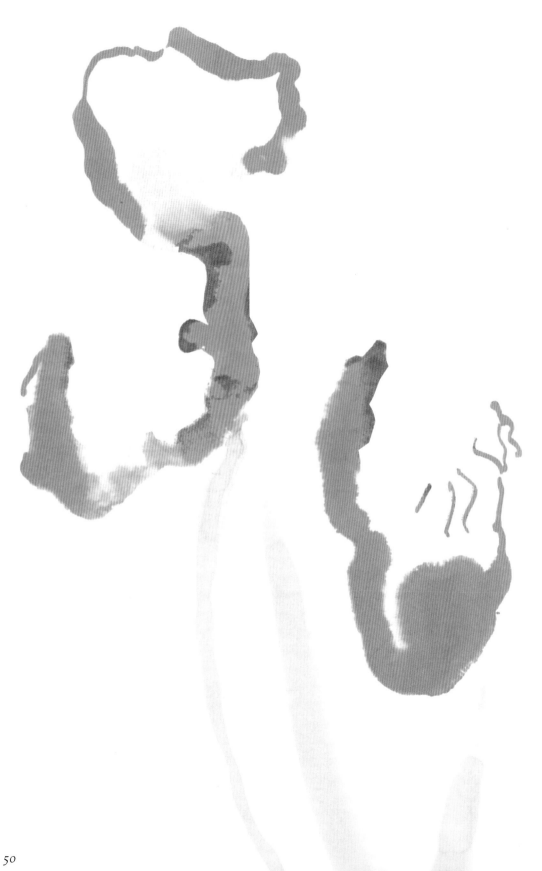

Youth
is
a
Gift
of
Nature.
Age is
a work
of Art.

Greeting Card Wisdom

Remember
to remember
the sweet things
that happen
to you.

Embrace Difficulty

After spending many years in deep exploration, the Buddha's first realization was that with life comes difficulty and suffering. Illness, old age, and death surround us. When we truly see, when we open our eyes and our hearts, we see all of the pain in the world.

One of the many paradoxes of life is that the more we open to our own pain and to the suffering of others, the more we can experience gratitude and joy. We realize that when we feel pain, at that very moment there are people with troubles and anxieties in our community, in our country, and throughout the planet who are also experiencing pain. When we understand that we are all connected by life's difficulties, we can begin to develop hope and true compassion.

If you think you're too small to be effective you have never been in bed with a mosquito.

BETTE REESE

A diamond is a chunk of coal that made good under pressure.

Love comforts like sunshine After rain.

Tears Are often
the Telescope
Through which
we see far
into
Heaven.

- HENRY WARD
  BEECHER

Right now
my life is
just one
Learning
Experience
after
another.

By the
end of
the
week
I
should
be a
Genius.

- JEANETTE OSIAS

Greeting Card Wisdom

A woman is like a tea bag - you never know how strong she is until she gets into hot water.

ELEANOR ROOSEVELT

Go beyond perceived limitations.

There is a story of a 36-year-old woman who was experiencing a major life transition. Ready for a career change, she was thinking of returning to college; she wanted to go to law school. Her dream was to provide legal counseling for low-income communities. And although going to law school to become a lawyer was what she really wanted, she explained to her mentor that she couldn't possibly achieve her dream. This path will take me six years, she exclaimed, By the time I finish law school, I'll be 42!

Her mentor responded, And if you don't go to law school, how old will you be in six years?

Life at Brush Dance provides us with many lessons in going beyond what we have perceived is possible. The Company literally began in my garage. When we were looking for space outside my garage, we were shown a building that once was a school cafeteria. It was enormous, long and wide, with very high ceilings. Quite a bit larger than my garage, I wondered how we would ever fill such a space! Today, one of our warehouses still occupies this space and Brush Dance has grown to occupy many times this space.

Recently, our ideas about limitations and perceptions have again been challenged. We are in the process of launching our Internet business, brushdance.com and our staff has doubled in size within a short period time. It is invigorating and scary at the same time.

It is intense, this focused gathering of ideas, people, and energy. Our business plan and strategy are clear. And yet I have no idea where this will lead!

Greeting Card Wisdom

show me
the person
who
never
makes a mistake
and I'll show
you the
person
who
never
makes
anything.

-UNKNOWN

Greeting Card Wisdom

Those who say
it cannot
be done

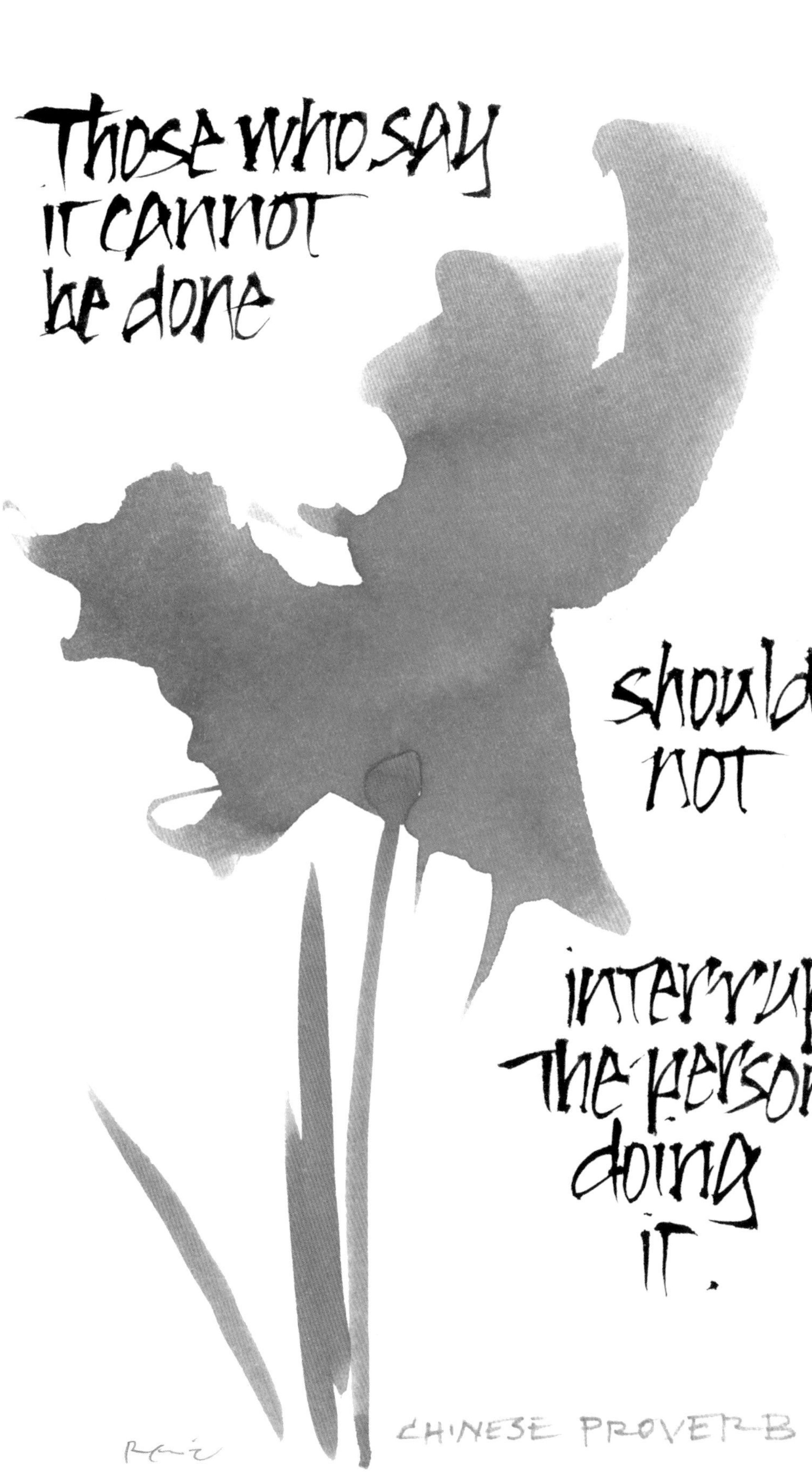

should
not

interrupt
the person
doing
it.

CHINESE PROVERB

Life is either
a Daring
adventure
or
nothing.

HELEN
KELLER
2002

Greeting Card Wisdom

whatever
you can do,
or dream
you can do,
you can.
Boldness
has a genius,
magic
and power
to it.

- G O E T H E

Greeting Card Wisdom

...and then the days came when the risk to remain tight in a bud was more painful than the risk it took to blossom.

ANAIS NIN

Greeting Card Wisdom

HURRAH !

I did the thing
I feared
the most.
Excuse me
while
I cheer.
Now here
I stand
a stronger
soul,
and all I've
lost is fear.

REBECCA McCANN

I get up.
I walk.
I fall
down.

Meanwhile,
I keep
Dancing.

HILLEL

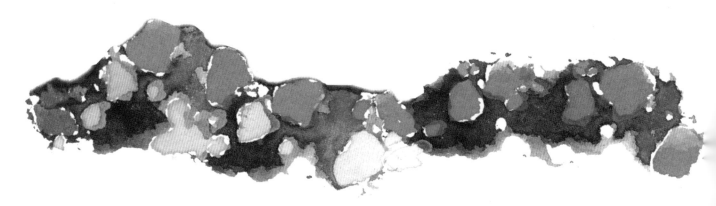

Greeting Card Wisdom

Take time to work.
It is the price of success.
Take time to meditate.
It is the source of power.
Take time to play.
It is the secret
        of perpetual youth.
Take time to read.
It is the way
        to knowledge.
Take time
to be friendly.
        It is the road
        to happiness.
Take time to laugh.
It is the music
        of the soul.
And take time
        to love
and be loved.

adapted from
AN OLD IRISH PRAYER

Greeting Card Wisdom

Follow your heart

A FEW YEARS AGO RENÉE SENT ME ONE OF HER BEAUTIFUL HANDMADE CARDS WITH THESE WORDS: LET US LIVE THE HIGHEST VISION OF WHAT IS POSSIBLE. THE MOMENT I SAW IT I KNEW THIS WOULD BE ONE OF OUR BEST-SELLING CARDS! IT WAS RENÉE'S WAY OF ACKNOWLEDGING OUR SHARED VISION AND MISSION TO CREATE PRODUCTS AND A COMPANY THAT OPERATE IN THE CONTEXT OF EXCELLENCE. OUR AIM IS NOT JUST ABOUT EXTERNAL SUCCESS; IT IS ROOTED IN THE DEEPLY HELD BELIEF THAT WE CAN EXPRESS WHAT WE VALUE MOST BY COMBINING POWERFUL, MEANINGFUL WORDS WITH ART.

AT BRUSH DANCE MY DAYS ARE A STEADY STREAM OF PROBLEMS AND CHALLENGES; I WORRY ABOUT PEOPLE, DEADLINES, MONEY, AND DOZENS OF OTHER THINGS THAT I SPECULATE COULD BE DONE BETTER. BUT EVERY SO OFTEN, USUALLY EARLY SUNDAY MORNINGS, I WALK AROUND OUR WAREHOUSE OF CARDS, JOURNALS, CALENDARS AND GIFT ITEMS. AS I SURVEY MY SURROUNDINGS, I THINK HOW LUCKY I AM TO BE CREATING PRODUCTS THAT TOUCH PEOPLE'S HEARTS! I TAKE A DEEP BREATH AND WONDER, HOW DID THIS HAPPEN? I AM FILLED WITH DEEP GRATITUDE AND AWE.

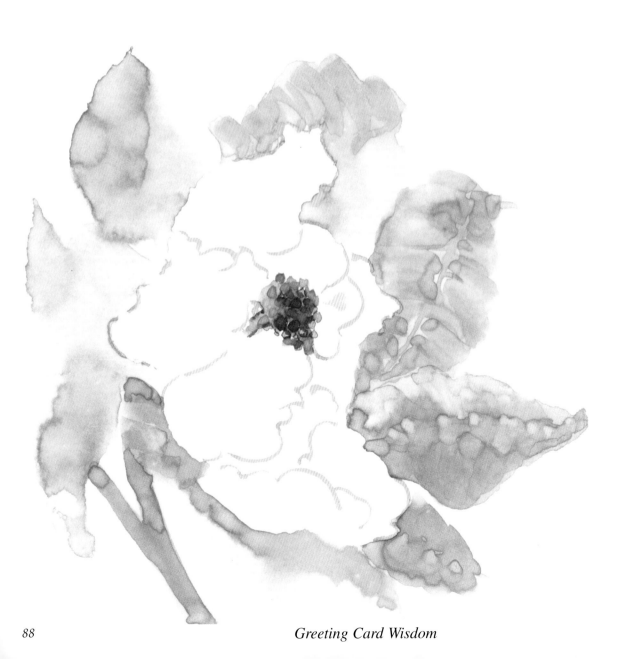

Greeting Card Wisdom

Greeting Card Wisdom

Follow your
Deepest Heart's
Desire.

Why
not?

Greeting Card Wisdom

Remember
four simple
words:
LIVE
LOVE
LAUGH
BLOOM

UNKNOWN

Greeting Card Wisdom

You will do
foolish
things
but do them
with
ENTHUSIASM

/COLETTE

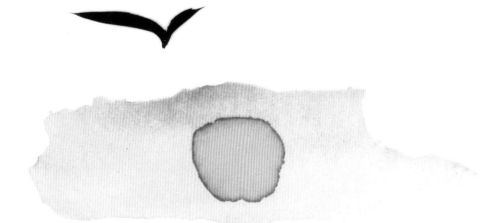

Let us
live the
Highest
Vision
of what
is
possible.

- INGA
GRACE

Value friendship and intimacy

Many years ago I spent some time with Harry Roberts, a teacher and mentor of mine. This was during a time when Harry was both aging and recovering from an operation. Harry had been trained by the Yurok Indians to be a healer. He was tough, and he was gruff — and he was also as sweet as he could be. He had a very direct way of expressing himself and relating to his life. He used to say, Life is very simple; all you have to do is answer three questions: What do you want? What do you have to do to get it? And are you willing to pay the price? I watched as a sly smile formed on Harry's face, as he added, Yeah . . . real simple.

The name Brush Dance came from a story told by Harry Roberts. At its heart, is a story about friendship and intimacy, a dialogue between a young boy and his uncle in which the boy is trying to understand the meaning of the brush dance healing ritual. The uncle explained:

The brush dance is a way to help a person in need. When a person is sick, with a sickness which people cannot see, it is then for that person we hold a brush dance. In the brush dance we sing fun songs and make jokes to let that person know that there is fun in the world. While everyone dances around the sick person, the doctor talks to the patient about what it is that troubles him.

When that person sees that friends who are singing happy songs to make him feel better surround him, then he feels that people care for him. He feels safe and tells the doctor what it is that bothers him, and the doctor tells the patient what he can do about his troubles. On the last night of the dance everyone brings out his or her very best costume. These costumes represent hundreds of hours of very careful work. They are made of the most rare and difficult-to-obtain materials. They have been kept in absolutely perfect condition. Never does a costume ever show any wear or that it has been used before. Everything is perfect. The costumes are the most beautiful things that an Indian can make.

Thus, when one dances before the sick person in this costume, it means that the dancer has cared enough for the patient to go to all of that trouble in the hope that he can help the patient . . . Now, how could I respect myself if I only went halfway or three quarters of the way to help someone? If I'm not going to help all the way, it is better that I don't go to the dance at all. So when I make a brush dance costume, the patient knows that I am going all the way for him. Then he feels reassured and will quite likely get well. This is what the brush dance represents. This is the way to be true to yourself.

Greeting Card Wisdom

A HUG
IS A
perfect
Gift,
One size
fits all,
and
nobody
minds
if you
exchange
it.

IVERN BALL

René

Greeting Card Wisdom

The best mirror is an old friend.

.LONGFELLOW

Real friends are those
who when you've
made a fool of yourself
don't feel
you've done a permanent
job.

JO
PETTY

Greeting Card Wisdom

FRIENDSHIP isn't a big thing— it's a million little things

UNKNOWN

Greeting Card Wisdom

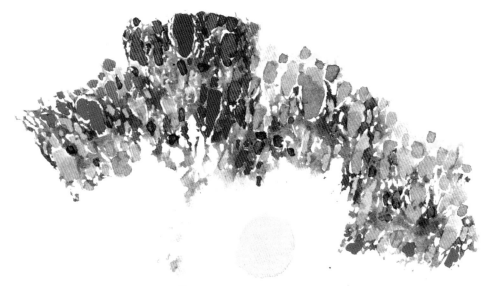

In every
woman
There is
a Queen.
Speak to
the Queen
and the
Queen
will
answer.

- NORWEGIAN
  PROVERB

.

Greeting Card Wisdom

Let Joy In

I will never forget a conversation I had with my daughter one day when she was about 10 years old. We were coming home from school, riding in my car, when she announced that when she was older and had moved out of the house, she planned to live nearby so she could visit her mother and me on Sundays. Immediately I become a little teary as I imagined my baby moving out of the house. At the same time, I was filled with joy at the idea that she wanted to live nearby so she could visit.

A few minutes later, I asked her about her day, to tell me something funny or unusual that happened, something that had made her laugh. She thought for a few minutes, and then she turned to me and said, Daddy, I laugh all day long!

As Greeting Card Wisdom was nearing completion, we met with Renée. The production, sales and design team gathered around a small table and we went through the book page by page. Ideas and creative energy were flying; everyone was participating and listening. From this collection of words and images, from these people working together, a book was being created. I trust that our joy comes through and brings you joy. I hope, like my daughter, you too can laugh all day long.

Where
you are
Joy
blossoms.

The best and most beautiful things in the world cannot be seen or even touched. They must be felt with the heart.

HELEN KELLER

ITS OKAY TO WAKE UP LAUGHING.

Angels can fly
because
they take themselves
lightly

GRATEFUL
ACKNOWLEDGEMENTS

- RENÉE LOCKS, FOR MAKING BRUSH DANCE POSSIBLE THROUGH THE INSPIRING WORDS AND DESIGNS SHE CREATES, AND FOR ALLOWING US ALL INTO HER GARDEN.

- JILL A. WEST FOR PROVIDING THE CREATIVE SPACE AND DISCIPLINE, FOR BEING OUR RUDDER WITH HER BALANCE OF HEART AND MIND.

- LISA DANKO FOR HER INSIGHTFUL DESIGN, TALENT AND PATIENCE.

- JEANIE BROOKE FOR HER STEADY EDITORIAL EYE.

- LEE LESSER FOR OFFERING HER TRUTH AND INSIGHT UNFLINCHINGLY.

- RUDY HURWICH FOR BELIEVING IN AND SUPPORTING BRUSH DANCE WHEN IT WAS JUST AN IDEA, AND FOR BEING MY MENTOR EVERY STEP OF THE WAY.

- PETER STRUGATZ FOR BEING A CHEERLEADER, VISIONARY AND FRIEND.

- ROB STEIN AND WARREN LANGLEY FOR THEIR TREMENDOUS SUPPORT, ENCOURAGEMENT AND GUIDANCE -- OUR LIGHTHOUSES -- ESPECIALLY DURING THE MOST CHALLENGING TIMES.

- BUD JACOB AND STEVE JACOBS FOR HELPING US ROW THE BOAT THROUGH DIFFICULT WATERS.

- ILENE LESSER, CHERI FORRESTER, MARSHA ANGUS, DEBORAH SHAMES, WESLEY KNITTER, AND LAURA ALDERS FOR THEIR IDEAS AND ENCOURAGEMENT.

- THE BRUSH DANCE COMMUNITY FOR THE INNUMERABLE SUPPORTERS AND BELIEVERS WHO SHARE AND ENCOURAGE OUR VISION.